YOUR KNOWLEDGE HAS VALUE

- We will publish your bachelor's and master's thesis, essays and papers

- Your own eBook and book - sold worldwide in all relevant shops

- Earn money with each sale

Upload your text at www.GRIN.com
and publish for free

Bibliographic information published by the German National Library:

The German National Library lists this publication in the National Bibliography; detailed bibliographic data are available on the Internet at http://dnb.dnb.de .

This book is copyright material and must not be copied, reproduced, transferred, distributed, leased, licensed or publicly performed or used in any way except as specifically permitted in writing by the publishers, as allowed under the terms and conditions under which it was purchased or as strictly permitted by applicable copyright law. Any unauthorized distribution or use of this text may be a direct infringement of the author s and publisher s rights and those responsible may be liable in law accordingly.

Imprint:

Copyright © 2009 GRIN Verlag
Print and binding: Books on Demand GmbH, Norderstedt Germany
ISBN: 9783668670082

This book at GRIN:

https://www.grin.com/document/418105

Tshewang Dorji

Gross National Happiness. Bhutan's Goal of Develpment

GRIN Verlag

GRIN - Your knowledge has value

Since its foundation in 1998, GRIN has specialized in publishing academic texts by students, college teachers and other academics as e-book and printed book. The website www.grin.com is an ideal platform for presenting term papers, final papers, scientific essays, dissertations and specialist books.

Visit us on the internet:

http://www.grin.com/

http://www.facebook.com/grincom

http://www.twitter.com/grin_com

Gross National Happiness (GNH)

"It is better to have milk and cheese many times, than beef just once." - Traditional Bhutanese proverb

1. Introduction 2
2. Gross National Happiness as a goal of development in Bhutan 3
3. Four Pillars of Gross National Happiness 4
   i) Sustainable and equitable socio-economic development 4
   ii) Conservation of Environment 5
   iii) Preservation and promotion of culture 5
   iv) Promotion of Good Governance 7
4. Conclusion 7
References 9

1. Introduction

Bhutan is also known as 'Druk-Yul', the land of the thunder dragon. It is located in the ridges of the Eastern Himalayan, with an area of 38,394 square kilometers. To the north lies China (Tibet) and India to the south. The country has population of around 650,000 (0.65 million) as per the Population Census conducted in 2005. Historians, experts and visitors often refer the nation as the land of "Peaceful Dragon" by the peace and tranquility that existed in the country for centuries.

Administratively, the country is operating under 10 central ministries, 20 districts and 205 blocks. All the regions have mystical landscape of pristine mountains and river system which demarcates one region (Block) from the other Blocks. Out of 650, 000 of the population, 69 percent of the resident population are located in rural areas. People living in rural regions are homogenous in the consumption as well as in production of agriculture goods and are culturally bonded with numerous believes and practices. Their life style are simple are mostly governed by Buddhist principles in their day to day activities.

The geopolitical condition, age old isolation policy and dynamic kings and leaders played an important role of protecting the country from foreign colonizers as well as becoming the casualty of any neighboring countries. Because of secluded isolation till 1960s and its rugged terrain Bhutan maintained a unique pristine culture, tradition based on Buddhist principles. Bhutan prides itself in its unique culture and tradition starting from dress (*Gho* for man and *Kira* for woman), food, language, dance, festival, sports, music, art, architecture, natural environment, and above all the development philosophy of Gross National Happiness (GNH), and many more. Buddhism is the state religion, though other faiths like Hinduism and Christianity exist. The density of population is 16 persons per every sq. km.

To maintain the sovereignty of state, Bhutan joined the membership of United Nations in 1971 under the leadership of the late King Jigme Dorji Wangchuck who is also popularly known as 'The Father of Modern Bhutan'. It was during his benevolent reign that Bhutan began its march to modernization and the first motorable road of the country was started between Phuntsholing in the South and Thimphu, now the capital city of Bhutan. There after the nation started moving forward at greater pace ranging from printing of its own currency with affiliation to the Reserve Bank of India.

In 1961 the First Five Year Plan (FYP) was launched to move towards development and modernization. The budgets were allocated in roads, transportation, education, health, forest and environment, agriculture, power and energy, animal husbandry, industries etc. The system of governance is in many respects unique in the world, providing people with direct access to the monarchy and a larger share on the decision making process because of the policy of decentralization and devolution of power to the people. Far-reaching initiatives were undertaken by successive monarchs to strengthen the kingdom's political and legal institutions and establish an effective democratic constitutional monarchy. Bhutan had its transition to democracy in March 2008 and at present the government is the first ever elected party, the Druk Phuensum Tshogpa and its President Jigme Y. Thinley as the first Prime Minister of Bhutan.

Bhutan's main human capital is clustered within the civil service consisting of 19000 civil servants as of 2006. The skilled labour comprises 20 to 30% of the total 19000. Skill labour shortages, rural urban migration, poor employability of job seekers, general apathy of job seekers towards blue collar jobs and poor working conditions are some challenges of human resource of the country.

Although agriculture is the livelihood of the people, the percentage of people working in secondary and tertiary sector is increasing. Its national income mainly comprises of hydroelectricity, tourism and forest products. The real GDP growth increased to 21.4 percent in 2007 from 6.3 percent in 2006 as per the national accounts statistics of the National Statistical Bureau due to the booming hydropower and agriculture sectors. The export of agriculture product and hydroelectricity to neighboring countries has increased drastically. But Bhutan imports almost all the technologies and petroleum products from neighboring countries especially from India.

Bhutan is a tourist hotspot and there are numerous opportunities in tourism industry and cottage industries to promote imaginative and creative innovation. Tourism can promote employment and income generation among the Bhutanese.

Basic education is class X and education is free. So also health is free. The Royal University of Bhutan is the only University which caters to higher studies within Bhutan and had 10 member colleges under its wings.

2. Gross National Happiness as a goal of development in Bhutan

Gross National Happiness (GNH) is the philosophy that embraces every aspect of development policies in Bhutan. It is based on the idea that a balance between spiritual and material development for its people is the middle path for development towards the attainment of happiness for its people. In short GNH means development with values. The concept of GNH as a unique and primary development philosophy was initiated and coined by His Majesty, the Fourth King of Bhutan, Jigme Singye Wangchuck. His Majesty believes that "Gross National Happiness is more important than Gross National Product" and therefore a people centered development with happiness as the end goal is what it should be for Bhutan. Karma Ura (2009) says that, the ultimate goal of development must be happiness and human well-being, but should not be economic development or to be a winner in the global competitions.

The Fifth King Jigme Khesar Namgyel Wangchuck, (December 17, 2006) further supported the through his address that, "...hence forth, our responsibilities will always be first and foremost, the peace and tranquility of the nation: the sovereignty and security of our country: the fulfilling of the vision of Gross National Happiness: the strengthening of the new system of democracy". The Constitution of Bhutan, 2008 clearly explains that the state will play the greatest role and carry responsibility in cultivating and promoting GNH as the main objective for public policies and plans for the development of country for all years to come. The Prime Minister of Bhutan, Jigme Yoezer Thinley is one strong advocate of GNH and has been sharing the vision of development of Bhutan at International Forums while equally taking strong initiatives at home to pursue GNH.

3. Four Pillars of Gross National Happiness

The success and attainment of happiness for all the Bhutanese lies in the strengthening of the four core areas termed as pillars. These pillars are as follows:

Four Pillars of Gross National Happiness (GNH)			
i) Sustainable and equitable socio-economic development	ii) Conservation of natural environment	iii) Preservation and promotion of culture	iv) Promotion of Good Governance

i) Sustainable and equitable socio-economic development

One of the main responsibilities of the government is to propel economic development in a sustainable and equitable manner. The benefits of development should be accessible to all the Bhutanese citizens. Thus, to improve the wellbeing of the Bhutanese the government commits itself to the development of the basic facilities that is fundamentally necessary. It reflects the concern of the government to improve the physical, intellectual, social and economic wellbeing of our people through the provision of free health care, free education, social and economic services.

Through its Five Year developmental plans and activities, sustainable and equitable services such as health, education, agriculture, energy, trade, commerce and industries, road and bridges, urban development and housing, information and communication, employment, tourism are developed throughout the 20 Dzongkhags (districts). Efforts have been made to reach these services to the people in the most remote villages of the Dzongkhags.

Beside, the Royal Government of Bhutan (RGOB) is aspires a self-reliant Bhutan, free from excessive dependence on foreign development assistance and Official Development Assistance. Bhutan tries to meet most of its developmental expenditures from its internal revenues such as from hydroelectricity, natural resources etc.

ii) Conservation of Environment

Under the far-sighted leadership of Their Majesties the Kings, conservation of environment continues to play a dominant and central role in their development efforts. In this regards, the government has formulated one of the most stringent set of policies and program to maintain harmony between human and nature, raise standards of its conservation practices on the face of rising pressure from urbanization, industrialization and population growth. The country's development processes are guided by the highest environment ethics, forsaking the short-term benefits, to ensure sustainability in the long term. The Constitution of Bhutan states that Bhutan will always maintain 60% of forest cover. Bhutan has 4 National Parks, 4 wildlife sanctuaries and 1nature reserve. Bhutan has been identified as one of the biodiversity hotspot of the world. King Jigme Singye Wangchuk was awarded the Champions of the Earth by the United Nations Environment Programne in 2005 to recognize his leadership in environmental conservation. 72.5 % of Bhutan is still covered with forest.

The conservation of the ecosystem is to ensure the very existence of nature. Conservation is also to prevent natural disasters that would bring suffering to the people and animals. Though there are no direct visible economic benefits, its conservation is a source of tourist attraction and thus revenue earner. Furthermore, the conservation of the ecosystem would ensure the continued flow of rivers and thus development of hydropower. Keeping in view the importance of the conservation of the environment, the National Environment Commission (NEC) reviews the project proposals and ensures that there is no large scale environment damage. The Nature Conservation Division (NCD) works closely with the NEC and other Non Governmental Organizations (NGO) in working towards conservation and promotion of the natural flora and fauna.

iii) Preservation and promotion of culture

Preservation and promotion of culture is said to be vital for the functioning of a harmonious and progressive society. One of the greatest strengths of Bhutan is its unique identity that comes from culture. For a country like Bhutan, which is small both in size and population, it is important to be different from others. It is culture that makes the Bhutanese distinct from the rest of the world. Thus, it is necessary for Bhutan to promote and preserve its spiritual and cultural values as it is the symbol of Bhutan and being Bhutanese.

The components of the pillar of preservation and promotion of culture are national identity, religion, language and literature, art and architecture, performing arts, dress, Driglam Namzha (righteous behavior aligning with the society towards harmonious living) , traditional etiquette, textile, sports and recreation. On the spiritual front many religious institutions are built, besides the renovation of some important monasteries.

King Jigme Singye Wangchuck in all his addresses to the nation and while visiting schools he reminds and stresses that "Being a small country, we do not have economic power. We do not have military muscle. We cannot play a dominant international role because of our small size and population and because we are a landlocked country. The only factor we can fall back on . . . which can strengthen Bhutan's sovereignty and our different identity is the unique culture we have". Therefore it is the duty of every Bhutanese to enhance and preserve its age old culture and tradition.

The Royal Academy of Performing Arts (RAPA) plays a key ambassador role in promoting Bhutanese culture around the globe. Preservation and promotion of religious mask dances, music and instruments, songs and dances are some of the main activities of the academy. The RGOB established the Ministry of Home and Cultural Affairs with the primary goal of preserving the culture and tradition of Bhutan. Most schools have a dedicated teacher to teach Bhutanese etiquette. The monastic body also plays a central role in preserving and promoting religious and spiritual culture of Bhutan. The Section 1 Article 4 (Culture) of the Constitution of Bhutan states that "The state shall endeavor to preserve, protect and promote the cultural heritage of the country, including monuments, places and objects of artistic or historic interest, *Dzongs* (fortresses), *Lhakhangs* (temples), *Goendeys* (Ten-sum, Nyes (sacred places), language, literature, music, visual arts and religion to enrich society and the cultural life of the citizens".

It is mandatory for all Bhutanese to be in formal dress, *gho* and *kira* and wear necessary accessories such as *kapney* (scarf for males) and *rachu* (scarf for females) during national occasions and while visiting offices and places of worship. Dzongkha is the national language and thus the official language of the country. The houses in rural Bhutan are traditional with modern amenities and buildings in the cities incorporate traditional Bhutanese art.

Similarly, the high tourist traffic of US$ 200 to 250 per day was introduced in Bhutan since 1961 in order to promote high quality tourist, with the policy of "high value- low volume tourism". Today tourism has become the second highest earner of hard currency in Bhutan beside hydroelectricity. The high value and low volume is introduced based on the principles of GNH to preserve and promote culture diversity of Bhutan.

iv) Promotion of Good Governance

Good Governance (GG) has four basic dimensions: anti-corruption, democratic culture, effective government and trust in institutional leaders. The purpose of GG is to bring about greater well-being and happiness to people. The Anti Corruption Commission was set up in 2006. Bhutan embraced democracy in 2008. The Officer of the Attorney General was established in 2006. The media expanded with GG is important to ensure accountability, transparency and efficiency in the country. One important aspect of GG is the promotion of decentralization to the grassroots. People get to decide their priority of development area and take ownership of the achievements at the local levels. The decentralization process empowered people and promoted balanced sustainable and equitable economic development.

The essential components of good governance included in promotion of GNH are the constitution, strengthening the government, decentralization support program, public service-back bone of good governance, auditing-towards greater accountability, pension scheme, foreign relations, judiciary, legislature, and national security. (Kuensel, Vol. XIX. No. 26, July 3, 2004: 1, 6-7). The promotion of good governance is also listed well in constitution of Bhutan.

The plans and strategies of all the ministries of the government must go through the GNH Commission to ensure that there is no conflict with the GNH principles. Any developmental policy that conflict with the GNH Principle is not considered as development policy in Bhutan.

4. Conclusion

The development philosophy of GNH is a unique ideology as is Bhutan too. However, it is not the uniqueness that arrests the attention of the international community but the approach Bhutan has taken. It is a great challenge for the government to ensure the conservation of environment with an ever-increasing Bhutanese population and therefore the need to expansion.

Urban sprawl, earth quake, storm, solid waste disposal, land degradation and pollution are some of the challenges facing the environment sector. Similarly, with the invasion of globalization, innovation and assimilation of culture and traditions, the task of the promotion and the preservation is big. To mention few, the western culture and globalization has deeply penetrated in urban areas victimizing vulnerable groups of children and women. The pertinent issues of drugs, street fights, prostitution, day-light robbery to name few, are the recent phenomenon becoming common in cities. Just before the third month of 2010, there were around 13 suicide cases of which five are students of 15 to 17 years old (Kuensel, SUCIDE RATE "ALARMING" March 4, 2010). With the increase in alarming suicide in happiness country indicates something must be wrong with our policy. Similarly, number of religious monuments called stupas and monasteries being vandalized by unprincipled people every year are increasing at an alarming rate too.

With the rise of such issues, GNH values should be well included in Bhutanese education system. A school is believed to be an extension of home and teachers are second parents to children. Teachers, parents and other stakeholders in the education of a child should be well informed on GNH and its values. GNH values could enhance in building a happy school with people promoting happiness to students and the community. Therefore in the beginning of 2010, "Education for GNH" has been commenced by the Ministry of Education and there was a conference and workshop on the theme. Schools have been provided with guidelines to infuse GNH values in the school curriculum and the school culture. School Principals and Master Teachers have been trained to lead the initiative.

Ronald Colman (2009) argues that, "GNH should have spiritual and contemplative education in a regular curriculum, with more environmental consciousness, critical thinking and cultural values into school curriculum". The Fourth King of Bhutan, Jigme Singye Wangchuck in his address to students on many occasions said, "The future of our nation lies in the hands of our children". By this, His Majesty meant that quality of education for the young Bhutanese is of paramount importance and that is the duty of today's parents, leaders and citizens to provide it (Ura, 2009).

The Fifth King, Jigme Khesar Namgyel Wangchuck rightly addressed on February 17, 2009 during the 3rd joint convocation of teacher graduates at Paro College of Education, "...parents and teachers, I want you to know that as King my passion will always be to nurture our youth, day after day, year after year – for it is their skills, their labour and commitment to the country that will build our future. There is no other path – no other tool – for Bhutan's future success. ―...Our nation's vision can only be fulfilled if the scope of our dreams and aspirations are matched by the reality of our commitments to nurturing our future citizens"

References

1. Bhutan 2020: A Vision for Peace, Prosperity and Happiness (1999). Retrieved March 24,2010, from http://www.gnhc.gov.bt/publications/pub/Bhutan2020_1.pdf

2. National Environmental Commission. (2002), Bhutan Road from Rio -National Assessment of Agenda 21. Retrieved May 1,2010, from http://www.nec.gov.bt/publications/RoadfromRio.pdf

3. National Environmental Commission. (2002), Middle Path, National Environment Strategy. Retrieved May 1,2010, from http://www.nec.gov.bt/publications/Middle%20Path.pdf

4. Penjor, D. (2008). Folktales and Educations: Roles of Bhutanese Folktales in value transmission. Retrieved January 20, 2010 from http://www.bhutanstudies.org.bt/admin/pubFiles/12-3.pdf

5. The Constitution of the Kingdom of Bhutan (2008). Retrieved May 1,2010, from http://www.constitution.bt/TsaThrim%20Eng%20%28A5%29.pdf

6. The four pillars of Gross National Happiness (July 3, 2004). Retrieved May 1,2010, from http://www.kuenselonline.com/modules.php?name=News&file=article&sid=4240

7. Thinley J. (1999). Gross National happiness and Human Development: searching for common ground: Thimphu: KMT.

YOUR KNOWLEDGE HAS VALUE

- We will publish your bachelor's and master's thesis, essays and papers

- Your own eBook and book - sold worldwide in all relevant shops

- Earn money with each sale

Upload your text at www.GRIN.com
and publish for free